My Very Own Bible

Stories retold by Karen Williamson

Illustrated by Hannah Wood

Retold by Karen Williamson
Illustrated by Hannah Wood

Published by Candle Books
an imprint of
Lion Hudson plc
Wilkinson House, Jordan Hill Road,
Oxford OX2 8DR, England
www.lionhudson.com/candle

ISBN 978 1 85985 876 9
e-ISBN 978 1 78128 030 0

First edition 2010

A catalogue record for this book is available
from the British Library

Printed and bound in China, April 2014, LH06

Contents

The Old Testament

The New Testament

The Old Testament

God Creates the World

In the beginning there was . . .
nothing.

Then God said, "Let there be light!"
And there was light. Day and night.

God put water into the sea and air
in the sky. Then he made dry land.
Beautiful flowers and tall trees sprang
up. He put the sun, moon and stars in
the sky.

God filled the sea with fish, the sky
with birds and the earth with all sorts
of creatures. Then God made the first
man, Adam, and the first woman, Eve.

God did all this in six days. It was all
very good. On day seven God rested.
No more creating!

That's how God created the world.

Genesis chapters 1–2

13

Adam and Eve Leave the Garden

God put Adam and Eve in a beautiful garden, called Eden.

"Eat anything you like," God told them, "but not the fruit from that special tree in the middle of the garden."

One day a sneaky snake slithered up to Eve.

"Why not eat the fruit on that tree?" he hissed.

So Eve ate the fruit. And Adam bit the forbidden fruit too.

That afternoon God asked them, "What have you done?"

"Eve gave me the fruit," said Adam.

Adam and Eve had disobeyed God, so he sent them out of the garden for ever.

Adam and Eve felt very sorry and very sad.

Genesis chapters 2–3

Noah and the Rainbow

There was just one good man left on the earth: Noah.

"I'm going to flood the world," God told Noah. "Build a great ark to hold your family and lots of animals."

So Noah and his sons built a great ark.

"Now take two of every creature into the ark," God told Noah.

So in went Noah, his family and all the creatures. Then the flood came. Soon the ark was afloat – with Noah, his family and the animals safe inside.

After forty days, the rain stopped and the water went down.

"Now you can all leave the ark," God told Noah.

Then God put a rainbow in the sky. It still reminds us that God saved Noah from the flood.

Genesis chapters 6–9

Joseph and his Brothers

Jacob had twelve sons, but he loved Joseph more than all the rest.

Jacob gave Joseph a fantastic coat. His brothers were very jealous. Why should Joseph get all the best things?

The brothers grew so angry that they sold Joseph to traders. The traders took Joseph to the far-off land of Egypt.

But after many adventures, Joseph became the king of Egypt's top man!

And one day Joseph's father and brothers came to Egypt to live too. How glad Jacob was to find his beloved son Joseph safe again!

Genesis chapters 37–45

19

The Baby in the Basket

The cruel king of Egypt said, "Throw every Israelite baby boy into the river!"

But one Israelite mother wanted to save her baby. She made a basket from rushes, laid her baby in it and floated it in the river.

When the princess of Egypt came to bathe, she saw the baby in the basket. She loved the little child and took him to her palace.

The princess named the boy "Moses" and brought him up as a royal prince.

So God saved this Israelite baby boy. He grew up to become the leader of his people, the Israelites.

Exodus chapters 1–2

Moses and Pharaoh

When Moses grew up, he went and stood before the king of Egypt.

"God says: 'Let my people go,'" said Moses.

"I don't know this God of yours," shouted Pharaoh. "And I'm certainly not letting the Israelites go free!"

But Moses came back time after time.

At last Pharaoh said to Moses, "Get your people out of Egypt!"

So the Israelites left.

Moses led his people out of Egypt on a long journey to a land that God had promised them.

Exodus chapters 5–13

23

Moses Crosses the Red Sea

When the Egyptians realized that the Israelites had gone, they were furious. They chased after them.

The Israelites arrived at the shores of the Red Sea: but how were they to get across?

"Don't be afraid!" said Moses. "God will help us."

He stretched out his hand – and the water divided.

The Israelites walked safely across on dry land. Then Moses lowered his hand and the water flowed back.

Now at last the Israelites were safe from the Egyptians.

Exodus chapter 14

Food in the Desert

Before long the Israelites ran out of food.

"Moses, why did you lead us into the desert?" they shouted. "We'll starve to death! We should have stayed in Egypt!"

"Listen! God will take care of us," said Moses. "Wait till morning – then you'll see something wonderful!"

When they woke up, the Israelites saw white powder covering the ground. It tasted good!

They called it "manna" and found it every morning.

God provided food in the desert.

Exodus chapter 16

The Ten Commandments

The Israelites trudged on for weeks through the hot desert sand.

At last they came to Mount Sinai, where they set up camp.

Moses climbed the lofty mountain to meet God.

"I will be your God and you shall be my people," God promised him. "I will give you special rules for living. Write them down."

So Moses wrote down God's rules on two big, flat stones.

We call these rules the "Ten Commandments".

Exodus chapters 19–20

Joshua Destroys Jericho

At last the Israelites came to the land that God had promised them – the land of Canaan. Now they had to capture the mighty city of Jericho.

God told the Israelite leader Joshua, "For six days, march your people around Jericho. On the seventh day, march around it seven times. Then blow your trumpets and shout. If you do all this – the walls of Jericho will tumble."

The Israelites did just as God told them.

On the seventh day the priests blew their trumpets and the Israelites shouted.

Down crashed the walls, just as God had promised.

Joshua chapters 5–6

Samson the Strong

Samson was very powerful. God made him strong to fight the Israelites' enemies, the Philistines.

But Samson fell in love with a beautiful Philistine girl called Delilah.

"Tell me what makes you strong," she whispered, "or I'll know you don't really love me."

"If someone cuts off my hair," he told her, "I'll lose my strength."

That night Delilah cut off Samson's hair and the Philistines dragged him to jail.

Later the Philistines threw a party. "Fetch Samson from prison," they said. "Let's make fun of him!"

Samson prayed, "God, make me strong again!" Then he pushed the walls – and the roof fell on the Philistines.

Judges chapters 13–16

Ruth

Ruth and Naomi were widows – their husbands had died. One day Naomi decided to go back to the land her family had come from. And Ruth went with her.

They went to live in the town of Bethlehem.

Ruth was a beautiful woman. In the summer she went to the field of a rich farmer called Boaz to gather grain.

"You're welcome to work in my field," he told her.

Boaz loved Ruth and married her. They had a little boy. This made them very happy.

Ruth chapters 1–4

Samuel Listens to God

Samuel was a boy who helped the priests in God's Temple. One night, he heard a voice call, "Samuel!"

He ran to Eli, the chief priest.

"Here I am!" he said.

"I didn't call you," said Eli. "Go and lie down again."

This happened two more times. Now Eli knew it must be God calling.

"Go and lie down," said Eli. "If you hear the voice again, say, 'Speak, Lord – your helper is listening.'"

Samuel went back to bed – and soon he heard the voice again.

This time he answered, "Speak, Lord – your helper is listening!"

And God spoke to Samuel.

1 Samuel chapter 3

The Shepherd and the Giant

There was a young shepherd in Israel named David. Israel's enemies, the Philistines, came to do battle and David's brothers went to join the army. One day David took some food to his brothers.

A huge giant called Goliath marched out from the Philistine camp.

"Who will fight me?" he bawled.

The Israelites were scared.

"I will fight Goliath, with my shepherd's sling," said David boldly.

Then David whirled the sling around his head and let the sling-stone fly. It hit Goliath and the giant dropped down dead.

Years later, brave David became king of Israel.

1 Samuel chapter 17

The Wisest King

Solomon became king of Israel after his father, David, died.

One night, God came to Solomon in a dream.

"What gift would you like most of all?" God asked him.

"Please, God, make me wise! I need to make good choices when people come and ask me what they should do."

God was pleased Solomon didn't ask to become rich.

"I will make you wiser than anyone has ever been," God promised Solomon.

So Solomon became the wisest of kings.

1 Kings chapter 3

41

Elijah Asks for Food

Elijah was one of God's helpers. One day he had nothing to eat. So God told him, "You'll meet a woman on the road. Ask her for some food."

Elijah did meet a woman.

"Can you spare me some food," Elijah asked her.

"I've just enough food for one last meal for me and my son," the woman told Elijah sadly.

"Cook for me first!" Elijah said. "There will still be enough for you and your son."

So she cooked a meal for Elijah, and then prepared food for her son and herself.

And from that day on, the woman and her son never went without a meal.

1 Kings chapter 17

Elisha Takes Over

"Go and find a man named Elisha,"
God told Elijah one day. "He will
become your helper."

Elijah found Elisha working in a field.
He put his cloak on Elisha to show he
wanted Elisha to be his helper.

After that Elisha went everywhere
with Elijah.

One day, all of a sudden, a chariot
and horses of fire appeared. They drove
between Elijah and Elisha.

Whoosh! Elijah flew up to heaven.
Elisha watched him go.

As Elijah went, his coat fell off and
landed on the ground. Elisha picked it up.

Now he had taken over from Elijah.

1 Kings chapter 19
and 2 Kings chapter 2

Elisha and the Pot of Oil

Elisha met a woman.

"I've nothing to eat," she said. "Just this one little pot of oil."

"Borrow lots of empty pots and jars from your friends," said Elisha, "and then pour oil into them."

The woman collected lots of jars. Then she started to pour oil from her little pot. It just kept coming! It didn't stop.

Soon she had filled every jar in the house.

So the woman started to sell the oil. Now she was able to buy enough food to feed her family.

2 Kings chapter 4

Naaman Washes in the River

General Naaman had a horrible skin disease called leprosy. People with leprosy weren't allowed to go near other people.

Naaman's wife had a maid. "I wish my master could meet the prophet Elisha," the maid told her mistress. "Elisha would be able to heal him."

So Naaman went off to find Elisha.

"Wash yourself in the Jordan River seven times," Elisha told him. "Then you'll be well again."

Naaman wasn't sure about this. It sounded a bit silly. But then he decided, "I will do exactly what Elisha says."

So Naaman went down to the river to wash. After seven times, the leprosy vanished. He was completely well again.

2 Kings chapter 5

Daniel and the Lions

King Darius chose Daniel to be his top man.

Then the king made a new law: "Everyone must pray to me. Anyone who disobeys this law will be thrown to the lions."

Some nasty men spied on Daniel.

"O king!" they said sneakily. "We've seen Daniel praying to his God. You must give him to the lions!"

Darius felt sorry for Daniel. But his soldiers grabbed Daniel and threw him to the lions.

Next morning, King Darius hurried to the lion pit.

There stood Daniel, safe and sound.

"I prayed – and an angel shut the lions' mouths," said Daniel. "They couldn't harm me."

Daniel chapter 6

51

Jonah and the Gigantic Man-swallowing Fish

"Go to the city of Nineveh!" God told Jonah. "Tell its people to turn their lives around."

But Jonah ran away in a ship!

God sent a wild storm that scared the sailors.

"It's my fault," Jonah told them. "I disobeyed God. Throw me into the sea!"

The sailors flung Jonah into the sea – and the storm stopped.

An enormous fish swallowed Jonah.

Jonah prayed, "Lord, save me!" – and the fish spat him out on the beach.

"Go to Nineveh!" God told Jonah again.

And this time Jonah did as God told him.

Jonah chapters 1–4

The New Testament

The First Christmas

Mary lived in the village of Nazareth. She was going to marry Joseph the carpenter.

One day an angel appeared to her.

"Don't be scared, Mary," said the angel. "I have great news for you! You're going to have a baby. Call him Jesus!"

Soon after, Mary and Joseph had to travel to the town of Bethlehem. It was a long way and they both grew tired.

When at last they arrived, all the houses were full.

Then a man saw Mary's tired face. "You can stay in my stable," he offered. So they did.

And there in his stable, baby Jesus was born. How happy Mary was!

Luke chapters 1–2

The Shepherds' Story

In fields near Bethlehem, some shepherds were minding their sheep.

Suddenly a shining angel appeared.

"Baby Jesus is born in Bethlehem," he told them.

Then a whole crowd of angels appeared, singing at the top of their voices.

When the angels had disappeared again, the shepherds left their sheep and rushed off to find baby Jesus.

They came to the stable, and told Mary about the angels.

Then the shepherds knelt before the little baby.

Luke chapter 2

The Wise Men's Story

Some wise men in a far country were looking up at the stars.

"Look!" said one. "There's a very special new star."

"It shows us that a new king is born," said another.

So the wise men set off to find this newborn king.

They followed the star all the way to Bethlehem, where at last it stopped.

There the wise men found baby Jesus.

They knelt down and gave him their gifts.

They gave him gold, and rich perfumes called frankincense and myrrh.

Matthew chapter 2

Jesus Grows Up

Mary and Joseph took Jesus back home to live in Nazareth.

When Jesus was twelve, they took him to the city of Jerusalem for a special festival. But Mary and Joseph lost Jesus in the crowds.

At last they found him in the Temple, talking to some teachers. The teachers thought young Jesus was very wise.

"Jesus, why did you get lost?" asked Mary. "We were so worried about you."

"I had to do my Heavenly Father's work!" replied Jesus.

Jesus knew that God had a very special job for him to do.

Luke chapter 2

John Baptizes Jesus

John lived in the desert.

Jesus came to John beside the River Jordan.

"Baptize me in the river," Jesus said. "It's what God wants."

"But Jesus, I should be baptized by you," said John.

"This is how God wants it," Jesus answered.

So John baptized Jesus in the river.

When Jesus came out of the water, a dove appeared above his head.

And a voice from heaven said, "This is my own dear Son. I am so very pleased with him."

Matthew chapter 3

Jesus Calls Four Fishermen

One day, Jesus saw four fishermen mending their fishing nets beside the lake.

They were Peter and his brother Andrew, James and his twin brother John.

"Follow me," said Jesus. "Then I will teach you how to catch people instead of fish!"

At once all four fishermen left their boats and followed Jesus.

They became some of Jesus' very special friends, his disciples.

Luke chapter 5

The Hole in the Roof

Jesus was telling stories to people in a house. Many wanted to see him, and the house was completely full.

Then four men came along, carrying a friend who couldn't walk. They couldn't get in. So the four friends climbed on the roof, tore a hole in it and lowered their friend through the hole.

When Jesus saw the man, he said: "Stand up! Pick up your mattress and go home."

Instantly, the man got up. He picked up his mattress and walked out of the house. He was healed!

The people were astonished. "We've never seen anything like it!" they said.

Mark chapter 2

Jesus Helps a Little Girl

Jairus was searching for Jesus.
He was terribly worried.

"My little girl is very ill," Jairus told
Jesus. "Please come and see her.
I know you can make her well."

On the way to Jairus's house, a man
met them.

"Don't bother Jesus now," he told
Jairus. "Your daughter is dead."

"Don't be afraid," Jesus comforted
Jairus. "Just believe in me."

When they arrived at Jairus's house,
Jesus took the little girl's hand.

"My dear, wake up," he said.

She opened her eyes and sat up.
Jesus had brought her back to life.

Mark chapter 5

Jesus Feeds a Great Crowd

One day Jesus was in the countryside, telling stories to people. They listened all day long. By evening, they all felt very hungry.

Nobody had any food – except one boy. He had five loaves and two fish. The boy gave his food to Jesus.

Jesus' disciples gave out the loaves and the fishes. There were at least five thousand people – but there was enough food for everyone!

There were even twelve baskets of leftovers.

People were amazed at Jesus' miracle, feeding so many with so little food.

John chapter 6

The Story of the Good Shepherd

Jesus told many great stories.
Here is one of them.

There was once a shepherd who had one hundred sheep. One night, one of his sheep went missing. Immediately, the shepherd went out to look for his lost sheep.

He searched everywhere.

At last the shepherd found his lost sheep. He carried it safely home on his shoulders.

"Come to my party," the shepherd told his friends. "I'm so happy that I've found my lost sheep!"

Jesus said, "God is happy too when anybody comes to him."

Luke chapter 15

The Story of the Lost Son

Jesus told another great story. It was about a farmer who had two sons.

One day the younger son left home. The boy journeyed a long way. He made new friends and gave lots of parties.

But after a while, the boy's money ran out. Now he had to work. He found a dirty job, looking after pigs.

He became so hungry that he ate the pigs' food.

At last, the younger son decided to return home.

When his father saw him coming, he was so happy! He threw a wonderful party to celebrate.

Luke chapter 15

Jesus Calms a Storm

One day Jesus was sailing across the lake with his special friends, the disciples.

He felt very tired and fell asleep.

Suddenly a great storm arose and the boat started to fill with water.

The disciples were very frightened.

They shook Jesus awake. "Help us, Master," they said, "or we'll all die!"

Jesus stood up in the boat. "Storm, be still!" he commanded.

At once, everything became quiet again.

The disciples were amazed! Even the wind and the waves obeyed Jesus.

Matthew chapter 8

Jesus and the Tiny Taxman

One day Jesus visited the city of Jericho.

A tiny man called Zacchaeus lived there.

He collected the tax money. No one liked him because he took too much money from people.

But Zacchaeus wanted to see Jesus. He was so small that he decided to climb a tree.

Jesus caught sight of Zacchaeus, balancing on his tree branch.

"Climb down, Zacchaeus!" said Jesus. "I'm coming to visit you."

And after Zacchaeus met Jesus, he completely changed. He even gave back all the money he had stolen.

Luke chapter 19

81

Jesus Rides into Jerusalem

One day Jesus and his friends went up to Jerusalem to celebrate a great festival.

On the way, Jesus told some of them, "Find a young donkey and bring it to me."

When Jesus' friends returned with the donkey, some of them spread their coats on its back. Then Jesus climbed on.

The donkey went clip-clop down the road, with Jesus on its back.

People cheered and threw their coats down in the road. Jesus' donkey trotted over the coats.

Then people started to tear down palm branches and wave them.

"Praise God!" they shouted.

Mark chapter 11

83

A Very Sad Day

But some of the people in Jerusalem hated Jesus. They wanted to kill him.

They trapped Jesus and took him to the Roman ruler, Pilate.

Pilate said, "Jesus hasn't done anything wrong."

But the crowd shouted, "Kill him! Kill him!"

So soldiers took Jesus and put him on a wooden cross.

They left him there to die.

Jesus' followers felt very sad.

They buried Jesus in a cave and rolled a huge stone across its doorway.

Mark chapters 14–15

The First Easter

Jesus had a dear friend named Mary. She went to visit his tomb.

Mary saw that the huge stone had been rolled away from the doorway. But she couldn't see Jesus' body.

She rushed back to find Jesus' friends in Jerusalem.

"They've taken Jesus' body," Mary cried.

Peter and John ran back to the tomb with her and looked inside. They saw the cloths that Jesus' body had been wrapped in.

Then Peter and John believed that Jesus had risen from the dead.

They went back home – but Mary stayed at the tomb.

John chapter 20

Mary Meets Jesus

Mary was crying. Then she noticed two angels sitting inside the tomb.

"Why are you crying?" they asked her.

"They've taken Jesus' body away," Mary answered.

Then she turned and saw someone standing near her.

"Why are you crying?" he asked.

Mary thought it was the gardener.

"If you've taken Jesus' body, please tell me where I can find it," she said.

The man just said, "Mary!"

It was Jesus!

Mary rushed off again to tell the disciples.

"I've just seen Jesus," she said. "He's alive!"

John chapter 20

Paul and Silas in Jail

Paul and Silas were followers of Jesus. They visited a town to tell everyone about him. But some people said, "These men are disturbing our city!"

They locked Paul and Silas in jail. But the two men spent the night singing hymns!

Suddenly the jail shook. It was an earthquake! The doors fell open and the prisoners' chains fell off.

The jailer thought everyone must have escaped.

"Don't worry!" said Paul. "Everyone's still here!"

"How can I be saved?" the jailer asked.

Paul explained – and the jailer believed in Jesus.

Acts chapter 16

Paul Goes to Rome

The Emperor of Rome didn't like Paul telling people the good news about Jesus. He had Paul arrested.

Paul had to travel to Rome by ship as a prisoner. But it was winter and soon the ship was caught in a great storm.

After many days, the boat was wrecked on an island. But God made sure no one drowned.

Paul started to gather wood to build a fire. A poisonous snake bit him.

But Paul wasn't harmed.
God protected him again.

Acts chapters 27–28